# Capybara

## The World's Largest Rodent

by Natalie Lunis

Consultant: Elizabeth Congdon, Ph.D.
Department of Biology
University of Missouri-St. Louis

BEARPORT
PUBLISHING

New York, New York

## Credits

Cover, © blewisphotography/Shutterstock; TOC, © ann&chris/Shutterstock; 4, Kathrin Ayer; 4–5, © Prisma/SuperStock; 6L, © age fotostock/SuperStock; 6R, © age fotostock/SuperStock; 7, © Doroshin Oleg/Shutterstock; 8L, © E. Sweet/Shutterstock; 8R, © Kenneth Murray/Photo Researchers, Inc.; 9, © Donna Ikenberry/Art Directors/Alamy; 10-11, © Konrad Wothe/Minden Pictures; 12, © Thomas Marent/Minden Pictures; 13, © Santiago Fernández/age fotostock/SuperStock; 14, © Tom Brakefield/Purestock/SuperStock; 15, © Elizabeth Congdon; 16–17, © Wildlife/Peter Arnold Inc.; 18, © kawisign/iStockphoto; 19, © Theo Allofs/Danita Delimont/Alamy; 20–21, © Wildlife/Peter Arnold Inc.; 22L, © Steve Raubenstine/iStockphoto; 22C, © Dan Bannister/iStockphoto; 22R, © Kobby Dagan/Shutterstock; 23TL, © age fotostock/SuperStock; 23TR, © Thomas Marent/Minden Pictures; 23BL, © Tom Brakefield/Purestock/SuperStock; 23BR, © ann&chris/Shutterstock; 23BKG, © Jan Gottwald/Shutterstock.

Publisher: Kenn Goin
Editorial Director: Adam Siegel
Creative Director: Spencer Brinker
Original Design: Otto Carbajal
Photo Researcher: Picture Perfect Professionals, LLC

*Library of Congress Cataloging-in-Publication Data*

Lunis, Natalie.
  Capybara : the world's largest rodent / by Natalie Lunis.
    p. cm. — (More supersized!)
  Includes bibliographical references and index.
  ISBN-13: 978-1-936087-31-0 (library binding)
  ISBN-10: 1-936087-31-6 (library binding)
  1. Capybara—Juvenile literature. I. Title.

  QL737.R662L86 2010
  599.35'9—dc22
                                                2009029847

For more information, write to Bearport Publishing Company, Inc., 101 Fifth Avenue, Suite 6R, New York, New York 10003. Printed in the United States of America in North Mankato, Minnesota.

082010
080910CGC

10 9 8 7 6 5 4 3 2

# Contents

# A Really Big Rodent

The capybara (kap-i-BAR-uh) is the biggest rodent in the world.

A capybara is the size of a large dog.

A capybara is about 4 feet (1.2 m) long. It weighs about 110 pounds (50 kg).

# Wet, Grassy Homes

Capybaras live in South America.

They live in grassy areas or forests that are near rivers, lakes, or ponds.

The places where capybaras live are warm all year. To stay cool during the hottest times, the large rodents rest in shallow water or in mud.

# Capybaras in the Wild

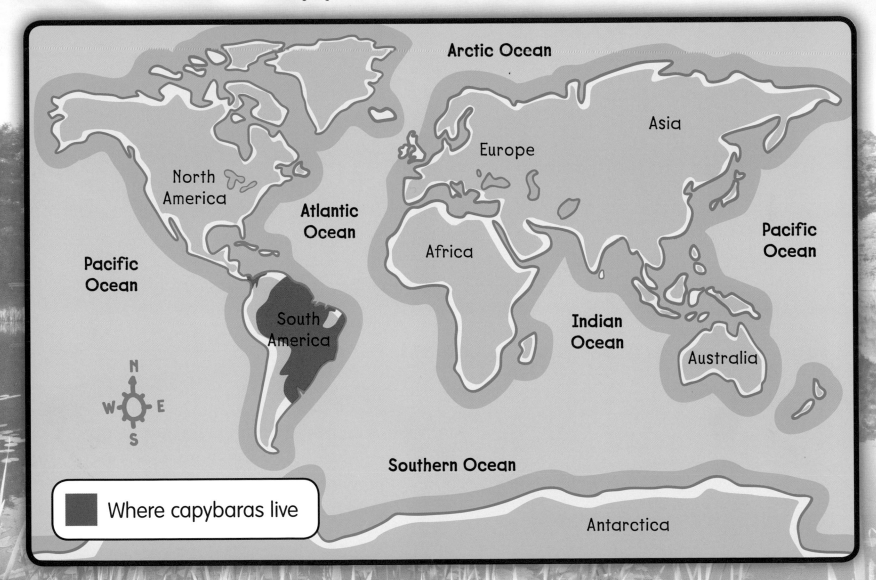

Arctic Ocean

Asia

Europe

North America

Atlantic Ocean

Pacific Ocean

Africa

Pacific Ocean

South America

Indian Ocean

Australia

N
W E
S

Southern Ocean

Antarctica

Where capybaras live

# Big Teeth

A capybara has long, curved front teeth.

It uses these big teeth to bite off and eat tough grasses and water plants.

A capybara's front teeth never stop growing. The capybara needs to gnaw on tough foods so that its teeth wear down and stay the right length.

front teeth

# Noisy Groups

Capybaras live in groups of 10 to 30 animals.

The members of a group live together in a large area.

They bark, grunt, chirp, and whistle to keep in touch with one another.

Sometimes groups of capybaras come together to form one large group of 100 or more animals.

# Bringing Up Babies

A mother capybara has a **litter** of four to eight babies.

The babies weigh about three pounds (1 kg) when they are born.

For the first few months of their lives, the babies' mother feeds them milk from her body.

By the time they are about four months old, the young capybaras start feeding on plants like the rest of the group.

baby capybaras drinking milk

All the female capybaras in a group help to take care of the young after they are born.

# Extra-Large Enemies

Because capybaras are so big, they don't have many enemies.

Some large animals, including **jaguars**, eagles, **caimans**, and snakes called anacondas, hunt and eat the young.

Only jaguars and anacondas hunt both babies and adults.

The jaguar is the third-largest member of the cat family. Only the tiger and the lion are larger.

jaguar

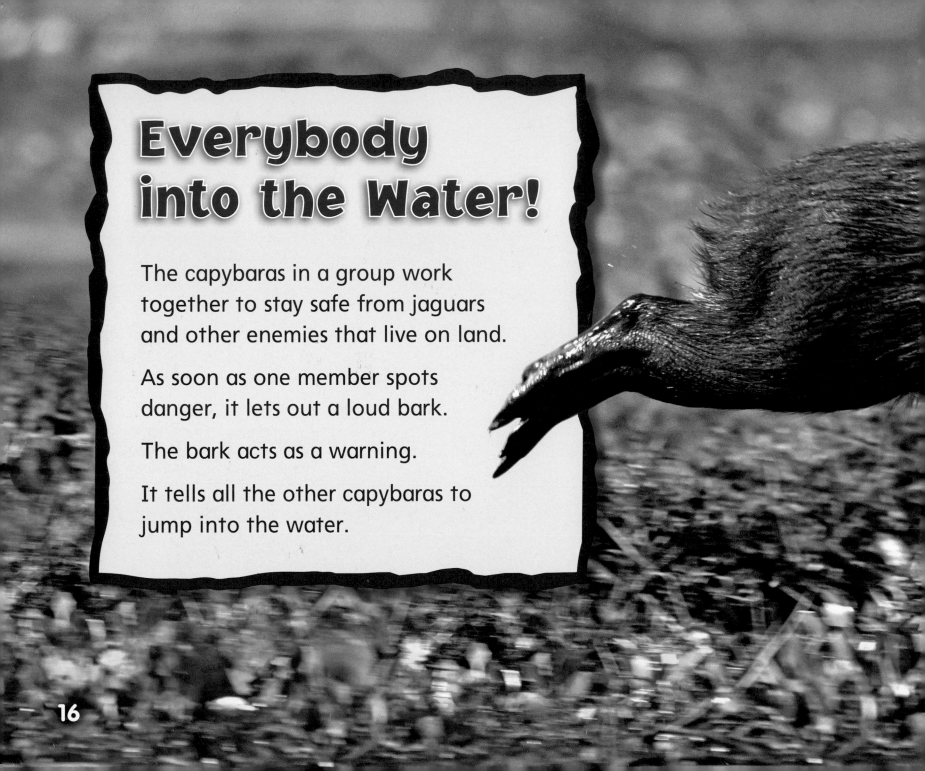

# Everybody into the Water!

The capybaras in a group work together to stay safe from jaguars and other enemies that live on land.

As soon as one member spots danger, it lets out a loud bark.

The bark acts as a warning.

It tells all the other capybaras to jump into the water.

Some members of a capybara group act as lookouts. Usually they are the first to see an enemy and bark a warning.

# Sneaky Swimmers

Capybaras are excellent swimmers.

To hide from enemies on land, they can stay underwater for up to five minutes.

They can also swim for hours with just their eyes, ears, and **nostrils** sticking out of the water.

This way, they can see all around— while their enemies cannot easily spot them.

webbed foot

Capybaras have webbed feet that act as paddles, helping the animals swim faster and with more power.

nostril

# Rodent Ranches

People have hunted capybaras for hundreds of years.

Now some people are raising them on ranches for their meat.

Surprisingly, this ranching is good for the future of the big rodents.

Large areas of the land they live on will be protected, instead of being drained for other kinds of ranches or farms.

As long as their wet, grassy homes survive, wild capybaras have a good chance of surviving, too.

# More Big Rodents

Capybaras belong to a group of animals called rodents. Many rodents, such as mice, rats, and chipmunks, are small—but some are fairly large. All rodents, including capybaras, have an upper and lower pair of sharp, curved teeth called incisors (in-SIZE-urz). These teeth never stop growing.

## Here are three more big rodents.

### North American Beaver

The beaver is the second-largest rodent in the world. A beaver can be 49 inches (124 cm) long and weigh up to 60 pounds (27 kg).

### North American Porcupine

The North American porcupine is about 35 inches (89 cm) long and weighs up to 40 pounds (18 kg).

### Mara

The mara lives in central and southern Argentina. It is about 29 inches (74 cm) long and weighs about 35 pounds (16 kg).

Capybara:
110 pounds (50 kg)

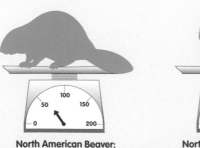

North American Beaver:
60 pounds (27 kg)

North American Porcupine:
40 pounds (18 kg)

Mara:
35 pounds (16 kg)

# Glossary

**caimans**
(KAY-muhnz)
animals that are
closely related to
alligators

**litter** (LIT-ur)
a group of baby
animals that are
born to the same
mother at the
same time

**jaguars**
(JAG-wahrz)
large spotted wild
cats that live in
Central and South
America

**nostrils**
(NOSS-truhlz)
openings in the
nose that are used
for breathing and
smelling

23

# Index

# Read More

**Kalman, Bobbie, and Reagan Miller.** *Guinea Pigs and Other Rodents.* New York: Crabtree (2006).

**Manera, Alexandria.** *Capybaras.* Chicago: Raintree (2003).

**Ricciuti, Edward R.** *What on Earth Is a Capybara?* Woodbridge, CT: Blackbirch Press (1995).

# Learn More Online

To learn more about capybaras, visit
**www.bearportpublishing.com/MoreSuperSized**